Jumpstarting Your Career: Tips & Hacks to Crack the Job-Search Code

Adam Najberg

Published by Adam Najberg, 2023.

While every precaution has been taken in the preparation of this book, the publisher assumes no responsibility for errors or omissions, or for damages resulting from the use of the information contained herein.

JUMPSTARTING YOUR CAREER: TIPS & HACKS TO CRACK THE JOB-SEARCH CODE

First edition. January 29, 2023.

ISBN: 979-8215753750

Written by Adam Najberg.

Introduction

Congratulations. If you're reading this, it means you're looking to take charge of your own career, to jumpstart it. I'm going to help you do that by cracking the seemingly impenetrable code. I'm going to offer tips to clarify an opaque process that heavily favors the employer. And through that, you'll start to identify some of your own advantages and gain confidence in crafting your own personal narrative, résumé and when you attend job interviews. Whether you're gainfully employed, looking for a job or wondering if you should change what you do to be more satisfied, we're going to start by stepping back and not falling into a pattern of actions designed solely for companies to get who and what they need, not one that was set up at all for your ease or satisfaction.

There are many resources out there, on LinkedIn, self-help blogs, "guru" websites and on the broader internet to help you improve your résumé. You can find thousands of free and premium résumé templates, subscription sites for résumé-building and sites that will build your résumé through artificial intelligence, or – for a price – a human being will do it for you. Maybe you have a friend who has experience helping others find jobs or have seen advertisements for expensive professional career and job counselors. There are bits and pieces out there that can help you, no doubt about it. But I've yet to find a single person or system that puts it all together, one that starts where most problems in the job-search process begin – and that's well before you ever think about writing a résumé or attending a job interview.

That's where I come in, and I hope you'll read on and let me help you and my method get you thinking and acting differently and more confidently as you look for your next job or to reshape your career.

I'm a public relations professional who spent 25 years as a reporter and editor, most of them at Dow Jones & Co., Inc. and *The Wall Street Journal*. I've been a boss since 1997, when I also started recruiting. I've sat on both sides of the interview table for three decades and conducted hundreds of interviews. I receive and read at least a half-dozen notes or résumés from job seekers each month. I've mentored nearly 150 people, cultivating young talent, helping mid-career journalists get to the next level or transition into news jobs in new industries. I've provided professional advice and confidence-boosters to everyone from recent graduates going for their first jobs to hardworking people who were laid off or downsized after over a decade at the same company or job, to C-suite executives who are looking to change their path and priorities.

I've offered my résumé-critiquing and career-advice services free for years via LinkedIn, but in the post-Covid world, I'm finding myself spread quite thin, with a lot of people seeking help. I continue to offer pro bono 30-minute consultations. And my friends will always have my ear. But I recently decided to "go pro" and offer a premium tier of paid services, including this ebook and related video series at a reasonable price, along with even deeper one-on-one, tailored service at a fair price for those who want to work with me over a series of sessions to get their business lives and career in order.

I am doing this because I really believe that the system of finding and applying for jobs is broken. It has become depersonalized, automated and saps energy and confidence from good, smart and hardworking people who can't figure out how to penetrate it in a way that makes it work for them. On the employer side, recruiters are overwhelmed by applications and have a hard time sorting the wheat from the chaff.

Advertising and applying has become so digitized and so easy, that very little thought now goes into the application process. And for employers, the sheer numbers of applications mean there's barely any time for brilliant assessments of skills and talent. I also believe that a résumé and interview skills are only end products that allow a job seeker to tell a clear, inspiring story about themselves and their skills and uniqueness. To get there, they first need to do a deep self-assessment, look back at who they are, their habits, attributes, skills and achievements and from that craft a strong professional narrative that is reflected in the résumé and job interviews they use to "sell" themselves to employers.

I know how difficult, discouraging and demeaning the job-search process can be and how overwhelmed you can get trying to sift through your long-term career prospects. Just remember, though, that no matter how many applications you have to lodge, no matter how often you're ghosted, most of it has nothing to do with you, and everything to do with a crummy, dilapidated system that has, paradoxically, gotten worse because of technology.

It's because the hiring process is supposed to be about human beings and people skills, handshakes, polite exchanges of handwritten notes and other forms of person-to-person contacts. Instead, it has devolved into a scummy soup of artificial intelligence and applicant-tracking software, recruiters-for-hire chasing commissions, six-second tests from overworked humans and other time-savers that have removed the person and personality from the process, anonymized it and turned it cold and uncivil.

I just want you to have some perspective as you look for your next job. Though you face long odds getting noticed through online applications, though recruiters and companies will ghost you, the odds aren't insurmountable, and there are ways to make yourself stand out to those reading your résumé that we'll focus on.

Also, another thing you need to keep in mind: As many jobs as there are on job sites and LinkedIn, remember that the best jobs will almost never be found there. We tend to get so fixated on the digital world, we can sometimes forget that we have personal and professional networks of real people we can tap for help and connections. Nearly every great job I've ever had has come from word of mouth or a friend or colleague connecting me to someone involved in the hiring process. It still really matters who you know, not just what you know.

That said, I'm not going to be able, in the space of these pages, to help you build your professional network, so we are going to stay within the confines of online job advertisements and the digital application and interview process, which is – for better or worse – mostly how jobs are sought and applied for in 2023.

I want you to stop thinking about the job-search process being about you searching for a job. If you are self-focused, you'll miss out on all of the important things that will help you gain an edge in the process. Start changing your thinking by putting yourself in the shoes of the recruiter and hiring manager. And when you do, the first thing you need to understand is most don't care that you're out of a job or need a job. They know nothing about you, probably wouldn't know you if you came up and tapped them on the back of the head. They certainly don't give a toss about your hopes and aspirations, so don't bother writing about them in your CV or in a cover letter or mentioning them at an interview. They mostly want an ass in the chair with the proven skills to do the job they're trying to fill. Many will not choose you to fill the job if they have any doubts about your skills or experience. While you do want to blow them away, do it by highlighting your demonstrated skills and how they led you to great achievements, achievements you can replicate for them and the glory of their team and company.

Lastly, remember that no matter how many applications you submit and never hear anything back, you only need one job. Don't take it personally. It's business, it's an unfortunate norm of today's high-speed digital world, and it's part of the process. If you come out of the process with a job you want, you've won.

I don't know exactly how others operate, but I'm not a "quick-fix" guy, and I'll never blow sunshine and rainbow unicorns up your nose or anywhere else. I'm not here to massage your ego. I'm here to offer up an honest critique of your résumé, help you craft your professional narrative, accentuate your positives and unique selling points, so you stand out in the job search. I don't just focus on your résumé or the color of your tie or dress for an interview, or how to answer interview questions.

My approach is 360 degrees, because I see job searches and career exploration as part of a unified and connected process – both an ecosystem and a game – where you can only succeed if you understand how to star in the role you're playing in that ecosystem and try to play the game at an expert level, though there are no exact rules. You're certainly not an equal in the job-search process, but you need to stop thinking yourself as completely powerless. You have to stand back and survey the entire landscape of applications, recruiters, company needs, how you position yourself through your résumé and your interviews. Create an image, then be that image. You have that power in you, if you change your perspective.

The job-search process is a lot about scoring points by rounding yourself out, choosing the right words, phrases and actions to make yourself stand out and avoid any egregious moves or faux pas so that you don't get points deducted or counted out. And, of course, there needs to be chemistry on both sides. The mistake a lot of job-seekers make is they are so desperate to get hired that they don't actually feel out the recruiter and interviewers or review the company and its culture enough to see whether they and the company are truly a great fit or not. So, even if you get the job, you find out it wasn't really what you expected or wanted, plus you don't like or fit in well at the company. Don't leap at the first thing that comes your way. Be calculating and methodical throughout the entire process, make sure every thought, every word on the page or every word out of your mouth is as measured and prepared as possible, though you never want to truly act like – or be like – someone else. You need to be yourself, just on a tighter leash.

Having a great résumé might get you invited for an interview, but if you suck at selling yourself and your professional narrative and anecdotes are not clear in your own head, you're going to fluff your interview. In this ebook, I offer you pragmatic, specific suggestions on approach, wording and phrasing, on actions you can take to improve your odds of standing out in your job hunt. I can also work with you to become more confident, make better decisions about what you want and take greater control of your career.

I break the process down into three parts; your professional narrative, your résumé and your interview. But what you'll realize, as you examine and reshape those three critical elements of every job search is not so much the end-product, but the self-awareness that helps you create the end product. I hope that as you go through and complete the steps of jumpstarting your career, you'll discover more about who you really are, what makes you great, special or stand out from others and what you truly want for your career. You'll come to understand how to present yourself in a way so that the messages you send are received the way you want them to be in both writing and in person. It's empowering to feel some modicum of control in an otherwise highly stressful and impersonal process, one that typically favors the employer, who gets to choose from dozens or hundreds of people for a single job.

If you prefer not to read this whole book or are more-visual in your approach, my video series, which I offer as a premium complement to this book, will also give you some specific suggestions on what to do to improve your résumé, your narrative and your job interviews. This ebook is much more-comprehensive and deeper, though. And if you want to do one-on-one sessions with me, we'll run through all of the above, plus do several back-and-forth rounds of résumé revisions, a mock interview, a critique of how you did and areas of improvement, along with answering other questions you have about getting onto the career path you want with the exact job you've been seeking.

A couple of final notes for this introduction: I'm purposely not including full sample résumés anywhere in this ebook, because – inevitably – the lazy will treat them as templates. As you go through these pages, you'll see I keep emphasizing how personalized your résumé needs to be to reflect your own narrative, tone, style and to fit the sector, company and types of jobs you're applying for. There is no "one-size-fits-all" template that does that, and I'd be doing you a disservice if I tried to create or share one with you.

Also, throughout this ebook, you'll see references to your résumé or your CV, which stands for "curriculum vitae." It's just another, shorter way to refer to the document. I use them interchangeably.

Part I
Crafting Your Personal Narrative

The Long Odds Against Getting Noticed – and How to Overcome Them

To apply for a job, employers will tell you all you need to do is submit your résumé online. If you just do that, fill it out and click on the "send" button, chances are very good that you'll never hear anything back from the company looking to fill the role.

Back in the day, when the world was analogue and more genteel, you found most jobs in the "help wanted" ads in your local newspaper. You wrote or typed up a cover letter, polished your résumé, submitted by snail mail, and a human being would either come back to you with a short, polite letter telling you that you didn't get the job, but they'd keep your details on file. Or, you'd get a note praising your qualifications and an invitation to an in-person interview.

If you are a bit older and feel the process has gotten less-personal, or if you're just starting to apply for jobs and find the process cold, you're not wrong. A few things happened that skew the odds of even getting an interview away from you. But we're going to spend a few minutes understanding why – and what you can do to counter that.

It stands to reason that when most jobs were advertised and filled locally that you'd have fewer people applying than today, when virtually every jobs site, including LinkedIn, is national or global. A junior-level job can easily attract over 1,000 applicants from all over the world, many of whom ignored the part that said "no relocation package," or "U.S. citizens and green card-holders only, we're unable to sponsor for this role." Even as you move up the career chain, a mid-level role that does offer relocation will have several hundred applicants. You will usually have a single recruiter who oversees the job posting you're interested in. It's great for employers, in terms of choice, but also kind of dumb because the sheer numbers make it almost impossible to conduct highly personalized quality control. And none of this is particularly good for you. Your résumé may never pass by a human eyeball, with some companies using artificial intelligence or applicant-tracking software to scan your CV for keywords and the type and amount of experience they're seeking, to weed out those who don't qualify.

Please don't find any of this discouraging or worrying. I'm only telling you so you understand the magnitude of the bad odds you're facing to even get noticed. If a recruiter has to go through 1,000 applications, each gets – at most – six seconds to impress the recruiter enough to keep reading your résumé or have it end up in the garbage. That's what we call the "Six-Second Test," and you'll need to pass it if you are going to get invited to an interview. We'll work on making you stand out. And sometimes, it's even easier to leap the AI barrier.

Start by Crafting Your Professional Narrative

That's why we're starting, not with your résumé directly, but stepping back and thinking more broadly about your own professional narrative, which will underpin the entire document and the stories you tell about yourself at job interviews.

Why? I was a reporter and editor for 21 years, 12 of them with The Wall Street Journal, so I'm used to writing all kinds of different stories. And I've been writing all of my life, so I can see stories in my head. In all that time, I've only had writer's block once, early in my career. When I finally cleared it away, I realized the reason I couldn't get the story onto the page was because I didn't know what I wanted to say. And when I forced it, I'd find that I had churned out bland, generic and boring copy. Do that for the résumé you use to apply for a job, and you're almost certainly ensuring failure. Most-important to me, is that before I ever put pen to paper or fingers to keyboard, I always visualize the top of each story in my head.

That's how I want you to think about your own story. Think about who you are and how you choose to be seen. That is going to be your first superpower in this job-seeking process. Now, I'm going to ask you several questions to help you focus and craft your professional narrative.

Those questions are:

- What three adjectives best describe the professional you?
- What are your top three skills?
- What are your top three achievements?

Your Adjectives Define You and How Recruiters Will See You

I've read many résumés and cover letters, where self-descriptions bury you in the banal. "I'm a self-motivated, hardworking, strategic thinker, blah, blah, blah." Who would ever describe themselves as unmotivated, lazy and only focused on short-term results? And why so many adjectives? You know what happens when you lard up your résumé with too many adjectives, many of them generic or vastly overused? You make yourself unmemorable. The reader gets overwhelmed trying to sift through the word soup and bragging, then quickly loses focus – and you lose your chance at getting invited for an interview.

I am a huge advocate of a one-page résumé, where every word on the page is precious. For that page, I recommend you pick three adjectives – and three adjectives only – that you, and those around you – think best describe you. Start in your own head, then go poll your partner, friends and colleagues, though remember to be discreet should a colleague want to know why you're asking.

I've been asked what are "good" adjectives? I don't think there's a hard-and-fast, "good"-or-"bad" rule for adjectives to use in a résumé, but you should choose carefully, thinking about how what you're trying to say about yourself will be received. And use some common sense. You want to be memorable – but for the right reasons.

For example, how do you think a recruiter will view a job-seeker who describes herself as "rebellious?" Yes, you might have created a conversation-starter and may stick out in the mind of the recruiter, but someone who is conservative, or working for a conservative company, may toss you out right away as being the wrong fit for the job. If you're trying to convey that you don't always follow every stringent rule to get the job done, maybe describe yourself as an "innovative" thinker, or if you want to say you know how to act out of the box, say that, or that you're an "unconventional" problem-solver. Set yourself up to be a unique and high-achieving hero in your own narrative.

I will not give an exhaustive list of what adjectives to use or not use, but look at some of the ones below and how they signal something positive and memorable, as opposed to others that are generic, flat or that might conjure up a negative connotation. Take your cues from this.

Adjectives that burnish your personality and professional narrative include:

- "driven" or "ambitious" (vs "hardworking," which is not terrible, but makes you sound like you're slogging and is overused).
- "creative" or "imaginative" (vs "skilled" or "expert," which are overused. If you have to say you're an expert or skilled in something, you'd better have degrees, certification and decades of experience and other data and proof points to back up the claim).
- "motivated," "self-starting" or "determined," (vs "dependable," "reliable," "punctual" or "loyal," because you want to show you are pushing yourself through

hard tasks and intend to accomplish, not just hitting the low bars of showing up and being on time).

- "organized" – I'm on the fence about this one, because some of the best low-achieving bureaucrats and technocrats in the work force are often well-organized. Same for "flexible," which can be positive, but might also be interpreted as lacking a strong moral compass or not digging in when you are certain you know the best way to do something.
- "collaborative" (vs "team player," largely because you want to portray yourself as a leader or equal partner, not just one of the team members).
- "good-natured" or "patient" are solid personality traits. They don't move the bar much higher, but especially for a high-pressure role or a leadership position, both of these are virtues and signal maturity.
- Avoid claiming you're "humorous" or "witty," under the premise of "show, don't tell." BE funny for a line or two in your résumé to make the reader laugh, rather than telling someone you're a laugh riot. And be prepared to bring some dry wit into your interview, but nothing knee-slapping or over-the-top. It polishes the claims about your personality and is often a sign of emotionally mature people who tap humor to lighten tense moments.

One thing to note: You don't actually need to repeatedly use the adjectives you choose to describe yourself in your résumé. Do drop them once, near the top, perhaps in your "about" or "bio" section, but don't feel obliged to keep reminding the reader how creative or innovative you are. Having them in the CV does matter, because of AI and ATS software or apps, but you don't need to repeat them several times. The best CVs are understated, subtle, intriguing, hinting at the traits that make you a highly skilled, successful achiever, not a plodding doer who is looking to plump up their bona fides with extra words.

Skills That Define You

How you describe yourself – your adjectives – are an important building block of your narrative, how you perceive yourself and how you get recruiters and hiring managers to think of you. Ultimately, though, potential employers want to see that you have the proper experience and skills for the job they're trying to fill.

It's important for your professional narrative and your résumé to showcase those skills. And I'm going to ask you to think carefully about how you approach your current and previous jobs and what your top three skills are that make you so good at it.

Some basic ground rules. Generally, nobody cares if you type fast or if you're good at MS Word, PowerPoint, Excel or other software programs or apps. These days, if you're in sales, marketing, finance or other departments that share data and information, you're expected to come to the job with decent knowledge of software tools. If you're a specialist in SalesForce or SAP or some other proprietary software that is at the core of your job and responsibilities, or if you code in an important language and are applying for a game-development job, those skills do matter and you should consider including them among your top three.

Reserve space on your résumé for the skills that are rare or set you apart from others, ones that enhance your entire package of offerings and narrative. For example, if you're in an international role, do highlight that you're multilingual near the top of your résumé, and you can list the languages at the bottom. Skills like that are what we call "hard" skills, like foreign or computer languages, coding ability or proficiency in SalesForce, which should be fairly obvious to include as at least one entry among the top three in your list. You study or train to acquire "hard" skills. You may have degrees or certification to prove your skills. Regardless, you either have those hard skills, or you don't.

And then there are your "soft" skills, which are harder, but not impossible, to measure or identify. Try to include demonstrable attributes, such as "leadership experience," "organizational know-how," "interpersonal communications," "problem-solving ability," "strategic thinking," "collaborative talent" and others you've acquired or learned over time. That's because you'll definitely need to give specific examples and explanations of all these "soft" skills in your résumé and professional narrative. If you claim to be strong in "organizational know-how," explain somewhere in your CV that you are comfortable identifying and working within a highly matrixed organization. If you have "leadership experience," tell the reader what type of leader you are (eg. "high touch"), how many people you've managed and whether you've done it locally, globally, onsite and/or remote. Drip the references and examples organically and tersely into the job accomplishments bullet points I'll show you how to write later in this book.

Be an Achiever, not a Doer

Once you've identified your adjectives and skills, it's important to wrap them together into an anecdote about achievements. Because key to making your CV stand out in a sea of too many is to portray yourself as a high-flying achiever, rather than a ground-pounding "doer."

Adjectives are the "what," and skills are the "why" and "how" of your professional narrative. Achievements are the "so what," which will tell the reader how you put your best traits and skills together to accomplish something strong, clear and notable.

The mistake most résumé writers make is to use valuable space writing out their job description, their responsibilities or what they did on a day-to-day basis at their job or for a project. There is no faster way to bury yourself in the masses of the unmemorable by coming across as a "doer," no matter how much you actually did. You always want to be seen as an "achiever." Why? Doers go home, achievers get invited to interviews.

The key difference between a doer and achiever has to do with a focus on results. A doer tells you, "first, I did this. Then, I did that. And finally, I did this other thing." Nothing there to signal how you did your thing in a notable or great way or what you achieved in the end to benefit yourself, your team, the company, etc. An achiever focuses on the accomplishment, providing a supporting number or piece of evidence, and then caps the assertion of greatness by providing valuable context. How could you not want such a results-oriented achiever at your company? Look at these two examples:

<u>Doer:</u>

I oversaw our annual client conference, helping craft and execute strategy to provide a full agenda for our top investors. Led the team that carried out logistics in multiple locations for the gathering.

<u>Achiever:</u>

Crafted and executed innovative strategy to educate, engage and entertain 600 high-net-worth clients. Brought in Mariah Carey, Mark Mobius and Jim Cramer as headliners – all within a sharply reduced annual budget. Attendance rose 30% over previous year, due to my three-person team's marketing and promotion efforts.

If you're a recruiter reading a hundred or more CVs a day, which entry and candidate would stand out to you? The doer's entry is bland and unremarkable, focused on the plodding actions, not the important results of pulling in headliners and drawing in a larger audience than a year earlier, as well providing the context that they did all this with a sharply reduced budget. If nothing else, this job candidate will be remembered as "the Mariah Carey guy." Even being remembered for that in a sea of CVs is pretty remarkable. And it leads to potential anecdotes and interview questions, as I'll explain in a moment.

Lights, Camera, Action: Tell Compelling Stories to Cap Your Professional Narrative

You've got your adjectives, your skills and achievements laid out. But you're not done yet. To put a cap on your professional narrative, you have to actually craft the anecdotes you're going to tell, ones which make sense and sound authentic and show your passion in both writing and in an interview setting.

Start by writing down the whole anecdote you want to tell a recruiter or interviewer. The entire story of how you, displaying the traits of at least one of your adjectives, and using at least one of your top skills, managed to overcome adversity, naysayers, self-doubt – whatever it is in YOUR story – to achieve top results. In our example above, the achiever who attracted headline talent and pushed up attendance figures with only a small three- person team and a tight budget, demonstrated she was "determined." That's one adjective she used to describe herself atop her actual CV. And she proved she could "think and act innovatively," which happened to be one of her top-three skills.

Bear in mind you will not use the full written version of your anecdote in your CV, nor will you tell the entire story as you originally wrote it. So, once you have it on paper or on a screen, read it aloud and time it with a stopwatch or timer app. This is where you'll need to test both your editing and acting skills. Because the trick is to:

- Get the story down to 60 seconds or less, which means you need to read it over and over, cut it down each time, boiling it down to the essentials of your adjective, skill and impressive accomplishment.

- You will want to portray yourself as a winning achiever who faced down adversity, stayed calm, learned something and got things done at a high level.
- Once you have that final version, work primarily on the delivery. Inject confidence, a bit of humor ("I told my boss I did a great Mariah Carey karaoke impression if the money didn't work" was our achiever's one joke) and – most-difficult and most-important – you need to practice telling the anecdote over and over again in front of a mirror, to your friends or partner.
- Each time, you have to tell the jokes and fill your voice with the excitement and passion as you had the very first time you told the story. You want to nail the joke so that it sounds natural and raises a smile or laugh.
- Passion and excitement are contagious, so if you feel them, chances are you can get your interviewers to feel similarly. I can help you with this. This is what you'll trot out at your interviews to crush them.

Nobody likes an arrogant jerk. It's 100% vital that you are the hero of your own anecdote, but be a humble, or at least a self-effacing, hero, one capable of listening and learning, as well as leading. You want the focus to be on the traits you showed in achieving top results, not how cool or amazing you were while achieving them and then bragged about them. Self-effacement is a great technique to dial up the achievements, while reminding the interviewer that you're a likable, easygoing, low-maintenance person who gets things done.

Also after you have really nailed your written/spoken anecdote, you will want to distill it back down further to just the essential adjective or attribute and skill used to achieve a great result. And make that a bullet point of one, maybe two, lines under your previous experience or job entry.

And you will want to do this for EVERY bullet point under your previous job entries. If you have three bullets for your current job and each job before that, you'll need to craft and boil down three great anecdotes. Because great résumés and great interviews rest on a foundation of great anecdotes, based on your adjectives, skills and achievements, all to form a strong professional narrative.

Part II
Buffing Your Résumé

Wow! All of this so far, and we haven't even talked specifically yet about how to write your résumé. I hope that, up to this point, you've at least absorbed the key points so that your actual CV will come together quite easily and organically. It will, if you first have decided who you are, what you want to portray about yourself and how to craft those into a professional narrative that helps you stand out from a sea of other job-seekers. If you present yourself as an interesting person with intriguing and worthwhile skills and things to say, you will be ahead of the game. And when you finally do sit down and put your résumé together, you just need to remember to carry all of this over onto the page. If you do, you stand a far-better chance of passing the "Six-second Test" with recruiters, getting them to read the whole document and maybe even invite you for an interview.

Chances are you already have a working document you call your résumé and have submitted as part of one or more job applications. Did you get the job? Did you get a rejection letter? Did you ever get any feedback? I ask this because it's increasingly rare to get acknowledgment from a company that they've even received your application, let alone processed it and reached a decision. That's partly due to the sheer number of applications received, because the bar is so low for anybody and their brother to apply for jobs online. But it could also be that the company doesn't want any back-and-forth or litigious behavior from job-seekers they aren't interested in. Just using anecdotal evidence from the past four or five years, candidates who aren't invited for an interview won't hear from a majority of companies they apply to online.

A decent company, one that treats job candidates with respect, will send you a brief, form letter via email to reject you, often saying they'll keep your package on file for possible future openings. There are still "white-rhino" companies, often smaller ones, which will come back to you with a slightly longer or more-personal note rejecting you. You still are unlikely to get genuine feedback, so if you ever get a highly personal rejection note with helpful thoughts, suggestions or any sort of an explanation about why you don't fit or what you're missing, treasure it.

In fact, the vast majority of us will never hear anything back and never know why we didn't get invited for an interview or weren't deemed suitable for the job. The anonymous rebuffs and implied rejections can be quite discouraging and off-putting, hitting your confidence and knocking you off your game. What I'm going to say isn't going to be hugely helpful or instructive, but it's all you can really do. First, don't take it personally. If it's any consolation – or maybe you take it as a greater insult – there are better-than-even chances these days that you weren't even rejected by a human. It could well have been the company's AI bot or app that crawled your CV and flunked you without a human recruiter casting eyes on the document. I recently had one job-seeker I was coaching – who was questioning why he needed to redo his résumé – tell me he thought he'd have better odds gambling and hitting it big in Las Vegas than finding a job through applying blind online.

He does have a point, and it's one I should clarify right before we begin the potential exercise in futility by writing a really strong résumé: The best jobs are not found online. The best jobs are not on LinkedIn, no matter how much LinkedIn tries to convince you they are. There is no secret market for great jobs, but if you spend any significant time in one field or profession, you should have spent – or make a pledge to spend – significant time getting out, reaching out, meeting people in your area. Get to know them, let them get to know you. That's, after all, what LinkedIn was originally supposed to be about, before it was invaded by the waves of salespeople trying to peddle Web 3 crap or looking for cold leads, the self-proclaimed marketing gurus who always know better and the fake-humble types, who want to look great and glamorous in the business world.

It's amazingly powerful to know people before you ever need them or ask them for something. It's even more powerful when you connect with them and ask, in a non-creepy way, what their pain points are and to let them know you're there to help if they need you. Share, sparingly, items you read in your field that you think might be interesting to them. And ask them if they are interesting, or to tell you to stop bugging them if they aren't interesting.

In short, a great network is almost always your best bet for finding a great job. Luck and timing play a role, too, but having a couple of hundred people who know you in your field increases the chance that something you're interested in is open and your contacts think of you when they know you're available.

Here, however, I'm assuming you have no network. We're going to start from scratch, building you a strong CV, one that you can convert into a longer, more-detailed LinkedIn profile, which you'll use to start building that virtual and real network online.

Back to your résumé and our discouraged job-seeker who wanted to go to Vegas and believed betting it all on red 13 would yield better results than getting a job with an online application. So many CVs fail the recruiter's six-second test for so many reasons. It's almost not worth it looking at the résumé you already have and previously used to apply for jobs, unless it landed you a job or netted you some interviews previously. Tell me if that was the case, because we'll kick off at a different starting point. Otherwise, rather than dissect and reassemble or patch up what you have, let's get a fresh start.

First, like building your narrative, you need to think about how long your résumé should be, what information you should include – and exclude, for that matter – in what order you present the information and what style or tone you want to adopt. The style and tone will depend on whom you expect to read your CV – your audience – as well as the type of company and job you're applying for. Style and tone do matter, but they're not the primary things we're going to focus on. Let's say we'll consider them later, or maybe next-to-last, in the process.

Keep it Short & Sweet

I don't really want to have a lengthy discussion about résumé length. Unless you're expressly asked or instructed to provide a detailed, multi-page CV, perhaps to list all of your academic or professional publications or patents, don't waste your time with more than a single page of 500-600 words. That's plenty, considering the first audience you have to get through is either a bleary-eyed recruiter who will not sift through four pages of "you," unless you're the second coming of Albert Einstein – and maybe not even then – or an ATS or AI program or app that's simply playing "keyword Bingo." It's just enough space to let you show you have the attributes, hard and soft skills, experience, achievements and education or training to do the job better than others.

Yes, I know you're terribly important and have worked at a high level for 25 years, yada, yada, but I want you to step back and reassess how you view your résumé. It is not a file or full dossier on your entire professional career. It is an outline of the career positives you choose to accentuate. It's a blueprint of what you have done that you're proud of and that makes you stand out among other candidates for the same job. The fact that you've taken the time and made great, filtered decisions to give your résumé a laser-like focus may even be noticed or appreciated by recruiters and interviewers.

A powerful résumé drops bread crumbs for recruiters and interviewers, intrigues them, tantalizes them, leaves them wanting to know more about you. Signal, indicate, be prepared to elaborate, but not in the CV, itself. If all you think about is yourself and what you want to say, you're going to more likely than not fail to write a great CV. You need to think of who is reading your CV, along with how and what they use it for to evaluate you. Length of your résumé is not a key criterion. Make your CV fit a more-telegraphic, bullet-point format, with you, the human job candidate, ready and willing to regale them and fill out the bullets with sentences and anecdotes. So, to finish where I started, stick to one page, unless you have a very, very good reason to go longer than that.

Let's assume a human will read your résumé, but we'll also be prepared for an AI bot to do it by ensuring we lace the document with enough keywords so that that bot will rank you highly. I read the other day that around 98% of Fortune 500 companies use some sort of automated app or process to narrow down the mass of applications they receive. More on that in a minute.

A Brief, Inspiring Bio Section Can Help You Stand Out

I didn't realize a short introduction of yourself – an "about me" or "bio" section – atop a résumé was so controversial. But I get the most pushback from job-seekers whom I'm helping with CV revamps and recruiters who read the documents.

From the recruiter side of things, while I just urged you to consider your audience carefully as you decide how to craft and organize your résumé and its contents, I also know that recruiters (and I've been one, myself) can often shift into autopilot mode, scanning and skimming virtually identically composed CVs at light speed, looking more to disqualify than include. As a recruiter, nothing knocked me out of my auto mode more than a CV that looked different from the others. It literally forced me to stop, blink, start at the top again. By then, the writer had already passed the six-second test. Even if I didn't end up putting that CV on the pile for further checks or invitations to interview, I absolutely took notice of the candidate and considered their résumé differently and more-thoroughly than others before and after. And nearly every time, what got me was a two- or three-sentence intro or bio that de-anonymized the CV and personalized the writer. In short, because they cared enough to want me to know certain things about them, I read what they had to say, and often read further, sometimes all the way to the end of the CV.

And if you're a job-seeker, how could you NOT want to go for that low-hanging fruit? If any questions you, I'd ask why is it not at all controversial – in fact, it's expected – to include a bio and self-introduction atop your LinkedIn profile, often much-longer than the 2-3 sentence flag-planting professional introduction I'm counseling you to use at the top of your CV. But it's ultimately your CV, so you can decide whether you want to include that section or not. If you do, the only place to put it is right under your résumé's header.

If you're applying for different types of jobs or jobs in different industries, or even at different companies, consider adapting, or at least fine-tuning, your bio statement and other parts of your CV to more closely fit the language and presentation and culture of the company you're applying to and the sector it's in. You do always want to be true to your adjectives and skills that build your professional narrative. But you might want to switch around which adjectives or skills you use first or second, or you might pull in the fourth-place choice if you think it more-closely fits with the company or job.

That means you need to research the company before you apply to the job. If you're trying to work for a fast-moving startup, for example, your long-term, methodical fact-gathering and analysis process might not mesh well with what the company needs for the job they're trying to fill. Or you don't want to go on about how you work around systems and processes to achieve results if you're applying for a job with a regulatory agency or a heavily regulated bank or insurer. You get the point: The full skeleton of your CV will always be the same, but the way you put the flesh on the bones can, and should, be slightly different for each job and company you're applying to.

What should a great bio or "about me" section look like? Here are a couple of different examples, each one setting a tone and style of its own for the rest of the résumé. You need to word your opening narrative in such a way that you set a tone of your own.

We'll start with the LinkedIn bio statement written by Laszlo Bock, Google's former chief human resources officer, now the founder of a couple of different startup companies. His statement is quite matter-of-fact. He doesn't need to impress anybody, because just seeing his name already does that. It's a nearly perfect example of a straightforward, "here's-who-I-am, what-I-do-and-what-I've-achieved" bio statement that leaves very little doubt about what's so great and special about him. I mean, what else could he say to prove he was – and is – at the top of his profession of hiring, recruiting and building the future of work. He even has a touchy-feely reference to "a little bit of love" to soften the whole AI, tech and science vibe. My only quibble is my BS detector went off when I read his reference to "synthetic data," though I was kind of intrigued to read on and understand what it is.

In 2017, Laszlo Bock co-founded Humu to make work better through machine learning, science, and a little bit of love. In 2019, he co-founded Gretel.ai, the pioneer in synthetic data. Laszlo Bock built and led Google's people function for 10 years, responsible for attracting, developing, retaining and delighting "Googlers." During Bock's tenure, Google was named the Best Company to Work For more than 30 times around the world and received over 100 awards as an employer of choice.

If I were to boil that down to an "about" statement on a CV, it would look like this, losing the third-person presentation – because your CV is about you and should be in your own, first-person voice, while LinkedIn profiles have evolved to now make it normal for both first- and third-person introductions and descriptions:

Co-founded two startups, one, focused on machine learning, science and a little bit of love, the other, on synthetic data. Prior to that, built and led Google's people function for 10 years, attracting, developing, retaining and delighting "Googlers." Company won over 130 awards as a top place of working during my tenure.

Here's an example of what I'd call an understated, but very solid, professional intro from David Da Silva, who's a seasoned account manager for the risk & compliance information product supplied by my former company, Dow Jones & Co., Inc. I like it for its simplicity. You read it and you understand this guy has serious chops in his field. He comes across as a competent "closer," someone to whom you could hand the keys, and he'll bring in the new business. He writes it in the first person, while Bock's was in the third person. Either works, just be consistent. A nice touch to include his ongoing MBA studies, which shows he's continuing to reach upward to improve himself. I read it and almost completely understand his adjectives, value proposition and skills. If I could criticize one thing about it, is I would love one strong and clear achievement to back up his assertion about helping companies increase revenue and improve efficiency.

Account Manager with over 15 years of experience managing enterprise organizations for industry-leading companies. I'm known for strengthening existing business-to-business relationships and forging new ones, developing and deploying solutions to help companies connect with their own customers better, increase their revenue and improve efficiency. Currently completing my MBA and working for global leader in news, data and risk and compliance solutions, Dow Jones.

A shorter résumé version would be like this:

Account Manager with deep background managing enterprise organizations for industry-leading companies. I strengthen business-to-business relationships and forge new ones, developing and deploying solutions for companies to connect with their own customers better, increase their revenue and improve efficiency. Currently completing my MBA.

Here's one more, one which is a bit louder and gaudier, arranged differently to include longer job descriptions and a list of achievements, but still not over-the-top bragging or annoyingly arrogant. It's from Betty Liu, my former deputy bureau chief at Dow Jones Newswires, a former TV business news presenter who in on her way toward becoming a tycoon in the media sector

Betty Liu is the Chairman and CEO of D and Z Media Acquisition Corp, a special purpose acquisition company (SPAC) focused on the intersection between media and technology. She was formerly Chief Experience Officer at Intercontinental Exchange

(NYSE: ICE) and Executive Vice Chairman for NYSE Group, a wholly-owned subsidiary of ICE. In both roles, Liu was charged with enhancing and innovating the customer experience across the entire organization, as well as helping elevate relationships with the C-suite of ICE's thousands of business partners. Prior to joining the NYSE in 2018, Liu was an award-winning business journalist. She most recently anchored the Bloomberg Television "Daybreak Asia" program. She also co-created and anchored "In the Loop" for 8 years on Bloomberg. Prior to the NYSE acquisition, Liu served as founder and CEO of Radiate. Radiate's content of empowering leaders with expert advice continues to scale through NYSE's platforms today.

There's a lot of good stuff in this entry, though I think it's about three times as long as it needs to be for a CV and about twice as long as it should be for an effective LinkedIn "about me" section. The length comes from the fact-packing and too much specificity for what's supposed to be just a short, "here-I-am" section. But it's bold and brassy, the achievements are top-quality and clear, and there is absolutely no hyperbole in it. Most importantly, though, it sounds just like Betty, who is bold and confident – and for good reason, with all of her career accomplishments. The one sort of weak part of the intro is the reference to her SPAC being "focused on the intersection between media and technology." Even as a longtime news guy, I have no idea what that means. An example of a product or service or platform to explain what the company does would have been better than the throwaway marketing phrase.

If I were going to pare this down for Betty, I'd go with something like this for her LinkedIn profile:

Betty Liu is the Chairman and CEO of D and Z Media Acquisition Corp, a special purpose acquisition company (SPAC) which looks at how technology can enhance media. Longtime, award-winning wire, print and Bloomberg TV financial journalist. She was formerly Chief Experience Officer at Intercontinental Exchange (NYSE: ICE) and Executive Vice Chairman for NYSE Group. Known for enhancing and innovating customer experience and creating strong relationships with ICE's thousands of business partners.

And this, for her CV:

Chairman and CEO of listed media tech company. Longtime, award-winning wire, print and Bloomberg TV financial journalist. Former Chief Experience Officer at Intercontinental Exchange and Executive Vice Chairman for NYSE Group. Known for enhancing and innovating customer experience and creating strong ties with Intercontinental Exchange's business partners.

Authenticity is hugely important in your "about" statement. So, think before you put pen to paper about how you want the recruiter and interviewers to perceive you. You're going to hear that a lot from me in this section of the book. Your CV needs to sound like you, be you. You need to be yourself, be authentic and consistent, so that what you present in a face-to-face interview never veers too far from what you wrote on your CV, in terms of your tone and style. And let your CV reflect your character. Pretend to be someone else, or vastly different from who you actually are, and you'll smell like a phony to the interviewer.

I know it's tough to be original, so if you're struggling about how to start or what to say, scan and peruse LinkedIn to see what others atop your field are saying about themselves and how they're saying it. I'm not suggesting you lift or plagiarize, but do feel free to grab some turns of phrase that you find relevant or elegant. Note how the best writers present themselves, their adjectives, skills and achievements. Draw inspiration from them and pull in elements of the best. After enough drafts, the wording, style and tone will be a mishmash. Keep writing through and editing and you'll suddenly find on maybe draft 15 that you've found your own voice.

Keeping Your Job Entries Tight

Once you have your professional narrative and the top of your résumé squared away, you'll find the rest of it pretty much writes itself. And we've already covered so much of the theory and approach, now we just need to focus on the content (what you say about your job and experience) and how you say it (your format). After your introduction of yourself, you'll start to list your previous work experience, starting with the most-recent or current job you have and work backwards. If you have a long and storied career, start to go shorter after you get past the third job you list and feel free to have only a single line for the earliest entries of your career, but don't leave out companies you worked at or jobs you held and the years you worked there. That establishes the length of your career and experience and ensures no gaps you'll have to explain in your career. However, if you're feeling that you may be seen as too old or too experienced for a role you're chasing, you might want to leave out a few of the earliest entries, and later, in the education section of your CV, eliminate the dates. More about that later.

For the job entries, there's no exact formula, but if I were to give you a template for job entries, it would look something like this, short, sweet, focused facts, figures, adjectives, skills, achievements and, at most, three bullet points:

*(Title)*Head of Internal Communications *(Location)*Seattle, WA

(Company) KaliumKT *(Dates)* June 2021 to Present

(Description) Led seven-person global team crafting and executing strategies for effective internal relations and messaging with key corporate executives and other senior stakeholders. Partnered with HR and PR teams, we craft communications, train, educate and inform 20,000 domestic & international staff about policy, important corporate news and information.

(bullet point reflecting your key adjectives, skill & achievement x 3, as below)

- Trained 25 managing director-level & above senior leaders in team communications over four weeks of onsite & remote sessions, finishing two weeks ahead of original plan.
- Developed innovative rewards-based system for group-wide customer-satisfaction survey. Participation rate highest-ever 94% vs 72% year-earlier & response time improved 33%.
- Built award-winning global content hub and newsletters customized through AI for our key six business units around the world.

You'll note that this entry contains a tight job description, hitting key points, but not overwhelming with too many facts or details, under the "less-is-more" mantra. Same thing with the achievements. The numbers are few, but they were carefully chosen. And their size, scale and impact matter.

Also, very important to use short, declarative sentences and active verbs. Don't go passive. "Trained," "developed," "built," all tie the action to you. Short and sweet. "Was responsible for isn't exactly passive, but it feels wishy-washy," and "was named team leader after overseeing successful customer-satisfaction survey" makes it sound like you are some disembodied spirit, instead of the actual brains of the operation who made the survey successful with your great strategy and execution.

If a recruiter reads this job entry, they'll come away with everything they need to know about the candidate's responsibilities and accomplishments, as well as the type of go-getter that you are. The way it's written, too, both leaves the recruiter wanting more and provides some bread crumbs for an interviewer to follow up with questions about each entry.

For example, as you prep for the interview, the way this was written, you probably can expect questions like:

- Tell me about this customer-satisfaction survey? Who was it aimed at? What were its goals and impact? Why did it matter?
- What do you mean "rewards-based system?" Did you basically incentivize or bribe staff to reply? Isn't that kind of an obvious, and costly, way to get staff to do what you need them to do?

Knowing that, you can prepare your sharp, 60-seconds-or-less anecdote for each bullet. You can talk about how you gave sight to the executives about how the rank-and-file view working at the company and assess the quality of bosses at the company. You can explain how you made completing the survey fun and engaging at a very low cost through a lucky draw or gifts donated by vendors or partner companies.

This is the "gaming the system" or working within the ecosystem I've mentioned previously. If you craft your experience and job entries in the right way, you'll almost certainly trigger interviewers to ask you many of the questions you want them to answer and are prepared to answer through your carefully prepared anecdotes that make up your professional narrative. Not every question will come your way, and you can expect to get others that aren't based on your CV, but we'll cover those later, when we talk about how to crush your interview.

Nailing the Education Section of your Résumé

Unless you're a rocket scientist, we won't need to cover more than a few basic concepts – and you won't need more than a few lines – to dispatch this section of your CV. List your college or university, if you went to one, the degree you received, any Latin or other notable honors others in the world will have heard of and the dates attended. That's it. You're wasting your time, the recruiter's time and space on your résumé if you do anything more than that.

Here's an example:

(*Institution*) Bowdoin College (*Location*) Brunswick, ME

(*Degree*) A.B. Degree in Asian Studies (*Dates attended*) August 2000 – May 2004

If you've attended, or graduated from, a really well-known place, expect it to be a topic of conversation, or if your interviewer is a fellow alum. Ditto for attending an obscure place or getting an obscure degree. None of this is bad. In fact, it can be quite good to kickstart the conversation, so I'm going to recommend you have at least one great 60-seconds-or-less anecdote about your educational experience on the shelf, ready to roll out if it looks like the interviewer wants to talk about your education. Make it a fun and interesting story – why you opted to go for a degree in art appreciation instead of the business degree your parents wanted you to study.

I figured I would be able to spend a lot of time staring at paintings while I was unemployed,

or something like that would be your punchline, if you can pull that off.

If not, don't bother. I do hope you know a bit about campus life and/or

some of the more-famous professors at the institution, if asked.

By the same token, feel free to poke fun at your obscure institution, if asked why you picked it. Making a bit of a joke about yourself humanizes you, as long as you have a good line, and it's not over the top. Like, if asked why you went to St. John's College in Santa Fe, NM to study their "Great Books" curriculum, you could note:

I thought to myself, 'where else in the world could I follow up two years of ancient Greek – a language nobody else actually speaks anymore – with two years of ancient Latin?'

But remember you're not at an interview to do stand-up comedy. Use humor sparingly as a conversation-starter or ice-breaker, and in ways that lighten a tense mood or break an interview from an aggressive or persistent line of questioning that is throwing you off your game. A mild joke, besides showing your personality and quick-thinking, can help to change the subject.

Enough about jokes. Here's a serious question I was asked: Should you include a "skills" section on your résumé? My answer is pretty much, "no," at least the way they're typically done. Most résumé writers tend to waste space with the banal and unremarkable. In 2023, typing 90 words a minute or knowing PowerPoint and Excel or other software programs or apps are not skills you should be highlighting, unless they are absolutely crucial to the job you're seeking.

For more-specific apps expertise or software knowledge, treat these as higher qualifications and include them in the education section of your CV, especially if you've done any extended or expert-level training or have a certification. For example, if you took multiple computer coding courses and know several programming languages, if you're hardware-certified by Apple, or you've been trained and certified in PeopleSoft or SAP, treat all of that as training, and turn your CV's "Education" section into "Education and Training" or "Education and Certifications."

Wrapping up Your CV with a Bang or a Whimper?

The answer to this question really depends on what's left that you have to say to a recruiter or interviewer. Honestly, most recruiters won't read all the way to the bottom of your résumé, so you should be thinking of it – and writing it – like a news story, in an "inverted-pyramid" format, one which top loads all key information. As you progress downward, each bit of information gets progressively less-important.

That doesn't mean no recruiter or interviewer will go all the way through, nor does it mean that you should assume what you include at the bottom isn't important in helping qualify you for an interview and the job. But don't waste space with trivial stuff. As with every line above, the bottom of your CV needs to count, too. Keep it tight and be selective.

If you speak several languages, include a "Languages" section, listing the languages you are able to speak, read and/or write. But be clear about your level in each area of the language and list any official proficiency test results or certifications you have. Point is, don't include the two weeks you spent learning Spanish while on a Mexico vacation, but do show to what degree the years you studied it made you proficient in speaking, reading and writing, as below.

Languages

Spanish (speaking – fluent, reading – professionally proficient, writing – intermediate level), French (TEF – level 5), Mandarin Chinese (speaking, reading, writing – native)

A word of warning. Never puff your ability. Always assume you'll be verbally challenged to show your proficiency claim at the interview and realize you may be asked to sit for a more-formal test in the near-future. Keep it real. Languages are a demonstrable "hard" skill. Either use very clear words or official test results or certifications to solidify your level of speaking, reading and writing.

The last section of your CV might well be a "Personal" or "Hobbies" section, but again, only if what you choose to include makes you notable. No, "likes long walks on the beach" entries. If you're a proficient (and/or certified) rock climber, if you have participated in multiple marathons or half-marathons or play sports or musical instruments in a band/group at a high or near-professional level, include all that by all means. If you are a certified personal trainer, an MMA fighter or perform in community theater productions, mention that. Be matter-of-fact about it, though, not bragging, to keep the arrogance-free tone all the way through your CV. If you played college sports, you can include that, too. If you have an unusual hobby, or a hobby which comes with an unusual backstory, that's also a great bit of information to set yourself apart in your résumé and interview. Like a former colleague of mine who did a very high-level, high-stress job and used crocheting taught to him by his grandmother as a stress-reliever in the office. You can just write that you like to crochet to relieve stress – and be fairly sure you'll get asked the question, "what's up with that?"

And then you're done with a draft of your CV.

Do bear in mind that your résumé is always going to be a work in progress, and that you will want to have multiple versions for different types of jobs you're seeking in different sectors, and even for different companies. Personalize, personalize, personalize. If you use the same, exact résumé for every job application, it's likely you've made your CV too generic. If you're checking out the websites of companies you're looking to join, if you read the job descriptions closely and you're meticulous and determined to get a job, how can you NOT pick out key bits of company culture, different wordings or quirks that you'll want to include on your CV to stand out to a particular company? At the very least, it's a great habit to develop, even if it's not noticed or directly appreciated by the recruiter or interviewer. You can always find subtle ways to point out your research in the Q&A section of your interview, so your research and personalization of the CV will not be in vain.

Last, but not Least

This brings us to the last three things you need to think about for your résumé: formatting, keywords and how your CV connects to your LinkedIn profile.

I'm going to start with keywords and connecting your CV to your LinkedIn profile, because they are very closely tied together. These days, it's hugely important to have a LinkedIn profile, one that is active, lively and laced with keywords recruiters and their AI apps and programs and ATS software can scan through to match you with jobs.

One immediate difference between your standard CV and LinkedIn profile, in many countries, is that your résumé doesn't typically include a photo of yourself in the U.S., Canada and other countries (though you will often find them atop CVs in

Germany, France and other parts of Europe and Asia). My only word on the photo is, "choose wisely." Obviously, you don't want a photo with you wearing beer goggles or partying it up. Pick a somewhat professional-looking photo of yourself. Maybe in an outfit that says, "office" or "professional," rather than, "I'm kicking it in Cancun." It can be light and somewhat playful, not hugely formal. Look for something that lets the light in your eyes or your personality shine through, one where you're comfortable in the setting and by being photographed. Don't go too far into the boring and overly serious range, don't use an event photo where you look grainy or are looking sideways. Remember, this is the first thing a recruiter will see about you, and we all know that people can often judge a lot from first impressions.

Here's the way I want you to think about your LinkedIn profile: Same principle as your CV, based on adjectives, skills and achievements to build the professional narrative. And you'll be using the same "code" in your job-entry bullet points that is tied to anecdotes underpinning your professional narrative. But, because you're on someone else's digital real estate, you have far more room than on a single résumé page. Mind you, that's not giving you carte blanche to write 1,000 words, but you can consider adding a sentence to your intro section, go a tad longer on your job description and your bullets. You actually get two bites at the apple to describe yourself. First, right under your profile picture, you can pick a few key words (not keywords) to describe or define yourself. My short description is, "head of communications, documentary filmmaker, former WSJ journalist, angel investor." Lower down, in your "About" section, you can cut and paste what you've done for your CV's top section and add a few ruffles and flourishes.

You also have the ability to "pin" some of your best work – articles you've written, articles that recognize you or show you've won award – near the top of your profile page in the "Featured" section to burnish your achievements. That's a big advantage to stand out. Use it. And you can ask your connections for professional testimonials at the bottom of your profile. Don't go hog-wild, but do ask four or five former colleagues or bosses to write something nice professionally about you, highlighting a skill of yours, a good adjective to describe your work performance or share an anecdote that highlights why you're so good and special.

While LinkedIn ostensibly exists to let you build a network with other professionals, it has essentially become one of the world's largest, most-unwieldy job bazaars and gathering place for cold-calling salespeople and marketers in the world. Amid all the fake-humble bragging, BS-ing from marketers, digital cold-callers seeking leads and other snake-oil salespeople pumping nonsensical Web 3.0 products and services, there are megatons of global job listings. Many of them are out of date, already filled, already sort of promised to someone internal or destined to be reposted multiple times – and you always wonder whether it's because the compensation stinks relative to the job's level or whether they simply can't find someone who ticks all the qualification boxes. And yet, as cludgy and imperfect as it is, you could spend an entire day on there, applying to over 100 sales or marketing jobs. But herein lie the two greatest problems for you, the job-seeker, with LinkedIn's job search and application function.

First, the entire process is stacked against you and favors the employer. The ease of the application process and the sheer numbers of people using LinkedIn around the world make it almost more-likely that you'll hit the lottery than find your dream job on the platform – if it's even there at all. So many people apply, that employers could fill the job many times over before even getting to your CV, in some cases. The flipside, though, is the sheer numbers also mean it's almost humanly impossible for a recruiter to read every, single résumé submitted. And that's the second problem: The numbers make the entire process very depersonalized and anonymous. It's why you seldom hear back from companies and why you almost never find out not just why you didn't get invited to an interview, but whether any sentient being actually looked at your CV and cover letter.

That's why keywords are so vital on your CV, but especially your LinkedIn profile, where recruiters will often apply ATS or AI software when searching for people to headhunt, or later, to scan résumés and profiles for the words that most-closely match what they're looking for. I hope none of this feels ominous to you, because it shouldn't. It's actually good news. Once you understand what you need to do, it's a fairly mechanical process.

You don't have to be an SEO expert or a genius to get the keywords on your CV and LinkedIn profile right. Go straight back to the job description and start highlighting or circling words in there that are repeated or that stand out. Look, in particular at the specific skills and experience the company is seeking for that role. And start seeding your CV and profile with those words. This is absolutely the lowest possible hurdle you'll face while searching for a job. If you spend 15 minutes doing your homework, you'll clear it – and the first round of screening – with ease.

Just to give you a brief example of how to pull out keywords from a required skills section of a job listing from auctioneer Christie's in Hong Kong, look below. I'm highlighting and underlining the words you should definitely pull and use to defeat the AI and ATS software screening.

Specific duties & responsibilities will include but are not limited to:

Content

• Guide the overall <u>strategy of content</u> by <u>social media</u>, <u>online editorial</u> and <u>video content</u> teams, ensure their strategy is realistic and achievable that supports and extends <u>marketing</u> initiatives. The <u>content strategy</u> must reinforce the <u>brand</u> and continuous evolution and review of the strategy is key.

• Has a deep understanding of the <u>social media</u> ecosystem and lead the team to develop innovative ways and <u>content</u> to engage with potential clients on <u>social media</u> platforms.

• Ensure all content is on-<u>brand</u>, consistent in terms of style, quality and tone of voice, and <u>optimized</u> for search and user experience for <u>online</u>, <u>social</u>, <u>video</u>.

Background, skills and areas that matter come across through repetition of the same words. You just need to ensure you have them at least once, maybe twice, sometimes more throughout your own "about me" and "job experience" sections of your CV and LinkedIn profile.

By the same token, you'd be well-advised to match up your job experience word choice with what the company expects from successful applicants. Look at the highlighted words below. Again, this is why you always want to personalize your CV for each job application, and to the extent that you can find the overlapping, common skills and attributes companies want, in your LinkedIn profile. If you're applying for too many jobs, you can't really do much with your LinkedIn profile personalization without making it read like a patched-together Frankenstein profile. I suggest applying to a few similar jobs at a time, peppering your LinkedIn profile with the skills and attributes most sought after by companies in that one sector, then readjust the profile a week or two later using keywords from another sector, as you apply to several jobs in that sector.

The Candidate

• Degree holder in <u>Communications</u>, <u>Media</u>, <u>Marketing</u> or related disciplines.

• Minimum <u>12 years of proven success</u> in creating <u>social content</u>, <u>media storytelling</u> and <u>communications plans</u>, preferably within <u>art, culture, luxury</u> industries with minimum <u>two years</u> in <u>managerial</u> role.

• Experienced with <u>China digital communications</u> including but not limited to activation of platforms, eg. <u>Weibo, WeChat, RED, TK</u> etc and preferable with <u>social CRM or e-CRM</u> experience

• <u>Detail-oriented</u> and ability to identify priorities and create a streamlined, efficient team to meet the business need.

• A natural <u>collaborator</u>, able to <u>partner</u> effectively with multiple stakeholders

• Excellent written, presentation and communication skills in <u>English, Chinese and Mandarin</u>

Formatting and Aesthetics

Now it's finally time to address things like formatting, fonts, extra sections and other aesthetics. You want this saved for last because it's like putting a coat of paint on the walls of the house after you've installed the pipes and electricity, spackling over the holes and installing the wallboard. You need everything else done first, but that doesn't mean you should skimp on or not consider the aesthetics of your résumé.

Formatting and font say a lot about you. But sometimes what they say about you may not be good. Like if you choose a flowery, cursive-style font that a bleary-eyed recruiter can't read in the six seconds they've given themselves to look at each CV. They struggle to make out what you've written, and you lose. Besides being a plain serif or sans serif font, whatever font you choose needs to be legible in both big and small point sizes. The standard font size on a CV is 12 point. If you're having problems packing all your information onto the single page, you could drop down to 11 point or as low as 10 point, but never go smaller than that, or you risk legibility issues.

The overall CV's appearance and structure on the page should also take into consideration who your audience is likely or intended to be. You don't want a boring, blocky document if you're applying for a graphic-design job, for example – unless you're trying to be counterintuitive or show that you have an "old-school" vibe in your work. If you're applying for a job as an analyst at an investment bank, you want a short, tight, easy-to-read font for recruiters who only care about your achievements and university grades.

To get more-specific, the Times New Roman, 12 point, is the most-commonly used font for résumés. It's a serif font, meaning the letters have little tails. Besides Times New Roman, other fonts that are somewhat common on CVs include Cambria, Garamond, Georgia, Didot and Book Antiqua. I'm a big fan of sans serif fonts, and it's no surprise that Calibri 12 point, in which this e-book has been written, is among the top sans serif fonts for CVs. Others that work are Verdana, Helvetica, Latha and Trebuchet MS.

You want reasonable left, right, top and bottom margins. The closer you get to the edge of the page, the busier your résumé looks. You're not fooling anyone when you pack an addition five lines and 100 words by extending your margins. I'm going to suggest you go with one-inch margins all around – left, right, top, bottom – and figure out how to make everything fit.

To make your sections pop a bit, use **bold text**, *italics*, ALL CAPS and maybe the <u>underline</u> formatting. How and where is up to you, but be consistent. If the first section name on your résumé is **About Me**, make sure the **Work Experience** section is also bold. If you use *italics* for job dates or locations, stick with that formatting throughout. Remember that standard text should comprise the bulk of your CV, with the **bold**, *italics*, etc formatting all there simply to highlight or draw the eye toward a new area, thought or section on your CV.

Now, get to it! When you have a great résumé draft ready, we'll move on to talk about how you can crush the job interviews that will start rolling in.

Part III
How to Crush Your Job Interviews

So, you wrote a great résumé, nailing all sections, picking all the right keywords, intriguing the recruiter and getting an invitation to your first interview. This is what you wanted, a pathway to a real job that you want. Now what?

Now, you need to bring it: you, your keywords, your authenticity, the tone, style, messages, adjectives, skill and narrative that got you past the ATS/AI software and the tired or lazy recruiter. You need to put it all together, give them more – the live version of what impressed them on paper.

Though we're in a post-Covid period, chances are still pretty high that at least your first interview – maybe more of them – will be done via Zoom or the ghastly, bloated MS Teams or some other virtual conferencing software. At some point, though, or if you're applying locally, you may be asked to do in-person interviews. There are advantages and disadvantages to each, which I'll cover in a minute, but remember that the principles, preparation and approach are quite similar for both remote and live interviews, which is why I'm not going to formally separate the discussion about how you absolutely kill both versions on your way to finding a job.

Time to Research and Prep

You'll know by now that my career-hacking approach never starts with the end of the process, in this case, the interview. Before you get to the interview you need to prepare, research, remove as much of the unknown as possible and replace it with what you do and should know, so that you can interview with confidence and speak with authority and clarity.

There's no script for an interview:

What I'm going to suggest to you below is exactly that – suggestions. You can prepare and plan, but as former boxer Mike Tyson once said, "Everyone has a plan until they get punched in the mouth." The reason for your research is to give yourself some comfort by creating a knowledge base and a basic plan in your head for how to handle things you expect to come at you during the interview.

Nobody can know whether they will, or in what order, or if something flies at you that has nothing to do with your interview prep. It's at times like that, where the unprepared will stammer or have nothing to say, looking like a deer in the headlights. Don't be that person. If you know enough about the company, the sector, the interviewer or the job from your web research, you'll always have something that can pop into your mind to change the subject with or to help you recover from a brain fart.

Get to know your interviewer:

You've presumably already Googled the company when you applied for the job and customized your résumé. You've also already decided that, at least on paper, this company and job seem like a good fit with the way you are and what you're looking for in a job. Now, though, you need to go deeper with your research.

Try to find out who, specifically, will be interviewing you. You'll want to Google them, look at any bio or profile of the person or people on the company website. Look for YouTube videos where they're sitting on panels and try to find out who they are through their LinkedIn profiles, publications on the web, interview quotes they've given and anything else you can find. Be warned that if you do not have a paid LinkedIn subscription, the person you're checking out on the platform can see that you checked them out. It's not a bad thing for them to know you're doing your due diligence, but don't revisit the profile several times over several days, or it will look like you're a creepy stalker. Take screenshots and study them offline.

Get a sense for the interviewer. Do they seem intense or easygoing? Softspoken or garrulous? Do they make eye contact, or stare into the distance, when on a panel? Did they write anything that demonstrates deep intellect or strong expertise in their field? Without being creepy, see if you can find public information about your interviewer or interviewers on Facebook or Instagram. Is she married? Does he have kids? Does your interviewer like to go ice-fishing or play soccer? Not that you want to use all the information, and you can't make your assessment 100% water-tight, but you give yourself an advantage and some level of comfort in what can be a nerve-wracking and stressful interview process if you have some sense of who and what type of person you're going to be facing.

Don't sweat it if you can't figure out who your interviewer is going to be. Focus instead on the company, corporate culture, job, how to answer the interview questions you expect to face and what impression you want to leave with the person sitting across from you.

The best interviewers will roll into the interview and make you do most of the talking. Those types of interviews will see you talk 75% to the 25% talking done by the interviewer. Most of the time, you're not getting the best interviewers, at least at first-round interviews. My advice is don't overtalk or overshare, if you have a big blabber. If the interviewer seems intent on telling you a lot about themselves, let them do it, nodding along encouragingly. Why take the weight if they are determined to do it themselves? Wait for them to ask you questions, then answer. Most interviewers who talk too much at interviews will take your nodding, smiling and eye contact as a sign that you and they have a connection and have hit it off, that you'd be a good fit and should move on to a second interview. That's the point, even if you didn't think that's how you'd get there.

<u>Know the basics of the company:</u>

- What exactly does it do?
- How big is it?
- Where is it headquartered?
- What do you know about the city where it's headquartered?
- Who is the CEO?
- How many business units does it have?
- What products or services is it known for?

It's not that you want to spew those memorized details back during the interviewer, but you sound smarter when you answer a question about how you'd feel about relocation to their HQ in Texas by saying, "Well, I know Austin is a very progressive city in Texas, full of culture. I mean, hey, SXSW is there. Who wouldn't want to live in Austin and work for a company with 50,000 employees in six countries?"

What you're ultimately doing is giving yourself an edge in a hyper-competitive process. Preparing and researching the company shows that you cared and signals your seriousness of intent and desire to get the job. If you impress in other ways, that edge might be exactly what gets you the job.

<u>Craft the List of Questions You Think You'll be Asked:</u>

Nothing is ever 100%, but if you've followed my method in crafting your CV and professional narrative and use some common sense about what typically gets asked, you won't have a problem either figuring out the questions you'll be asked at your interview and how to answer them.

You also need to understand the approach and mentality of recruiters and interviewers doing early-round interviews, especially. While the company has whittled down the 1,000 applications to 20 people invited for first-round interviews, that's still a lot of people and hours spent deciding whether someone is strong and appealing enough pass through to the next round. And, you can assume the one opening you've applied for isn't the only thing the recruiter or interviewer is worried about. They likely have fulltime day jobs that eat up a lot of their time.

Point is: Don't expect an interviewer, at least in the first round, to have meticulously prepared for your interview. In fact, count on their not having done so, but plan for the eventuality that your interviewer is an outlier who did prepare thoroughly to grill you.

For the overworked interviewer, they might take a full day to conduct several interviews in a row. They'll typically print out your CV and those of the other interviewees, slip them into a folder or onto a clipboard, or maybe save them all to their iPad. But if they're doing five or six interviews in a single day, it's a lot, and the names and people run together.

Chances are good that a tight, one-page résumé full of tantalizing bits of information about the candidate is going to be too hard for them to resist. They'll look at your two-line bullet points for each of your job entries and focus on either trying to trip you up or get you to fill in the details. Either way, you win. You gamed them into asking you what you wanted to be asked about and what you are prepared to talk about. Let your 60-second anecdotes roll off your tongue, full of passion and other emotions.

It would be great if that's all you were asked, but most interviews tend to start with the interviewer introducing themselves and then asking you to do the same, followed by a quick rundown of the job description and the company's background and needs in filling the role. The interviewer then starts the questioning. They'll use your "about" statement and work experience to ask you questions. But inevitably, here are some of the questions not about your CV which you can expect, and a bit lower down, we'll craft some answers you can use or adapt to fit your own tone, style and narrative.

- What makes you think you're the best candidate for this job?

- What about this job is most-appealing to you?
- You've never done a job this big before. Why do you think you're ready for a step up?
- How have you dealt with a difficult boss or colleague, one who doesn't listen to you, or has a temper or bad attitude?
- How have you handled a challenging or difficult situation, where the odds were against your achieving the results you were asked to achieve?" or "Give an example of how you deal with adversity at work.
- Do you work better on your own, or do you prefer collaboration?
- This job isn't a natural fit for your skill set. What makes you think you'll be capable of doing it?
- Where do you see yourself in five years?"
- If we picked someone else for this job, would you consider another role at our company?
- If you got this job, what would your plan be to set yourself, and the company, up for success in the first several months?
- Can you share a situation where you were wrong, or made a mistake, that hurt your team or your project? How did you deal with that tough situation?
- You seem to have a knack for overachieving on your KPI and P&L. How can we be sure that will be the case here? Do you offer any guarantees? And what should we do with you if you don't overachieve here, as you have elsewhere?"

Especially at sales jobs, you might get asked to demonstrate how you'd sell something, rather than just talking about it from your CV. An interviewer could pull out a writing implement and ask you to "sell me this pen!"

I've also heard from more than one job candidate for banking and investment banking jobs warn that some interviewers can become combative or aggressive to see how you handle the stress, with questions like

- Why should we hire someone who studied at a second-tier college like you did?

Coming up with Answers to the Anticipated Questions:

The above list of what you might be asked is not exhaustive. Always expect a curve ball or two, maybe a stress question. But remember to breathe and that you know your own narrative best. Once you realize you actually know way more about yourself than the interviewer, you can use techniques, like changing the subject back to a line on your CV or parrying by asking the interviewer to explain what they mean in more detail, to buy yourself some time to come up with an answer. Because thinking on your feet is a skill you will need to develop and employ to be the best interviewee you can be. Treat every interview as a chance to polish that skill.

Now, let's get to answering those questions that don't come from your CV.

- What makes you think you're the best candidate for this job?

There are a couple ways to approach this first question. If you are not hugely experienced, or if the job is clearly a step up, don't oversell your experience and focus on what's new, different and special about you. Tell the interviewer about how most people in the field for a long time have a certain, standard approach to addressing industry challenges, presenting yourself as a next-generation thinker who has a new and innovative way of tackling them. And give an example or two of "old, standard" thinking vs your "new, innovative" thinking. Don't BS your way through if you don't have an example.

Or, if you are majorly experienced, push that angle. You have the knowledge, have put in the time and have pretty much seen and dealt with some of the worst, most-difficult stuff anyone could imagine, and you've succeeded through it all. Play up the hard work and learning, so that you come across as humble, not a braggart.

- What about this job is most-appealing to you?

Pick one aspect of the job and give yourself 60 seconds or less to expound on why that aspect is so great and interesting to you. A marketing role at a beverage company? "Just like Coca-Cola, I see our competition not just as company A, B or C, but the water coming out of everyone's faucet. I relish the challenge of making the value proposition of our drink so obvious to everyone out there that they won't even think of turning on the tap."

- You've never done a job this big before. Why do you

think you're ready for a step up?

This is similar to the first question. If you can't win on experience, win on innovation. Present yourself as an out-of-the-box thinker with a new approach, and give a strong example of how you've done this before. And let them know that, "you can pick someone who has been here before, but they won't give you anything you haven't already seen. The only thing I can promise you is that a lot of what I will do for your company is going to be new, different, innovative and highly successful. It won't be easy, and I'm not going to tell you every move I make will be 100% correct. But I don't come to this job with a closed mind or a set of textbook rules of how to do the job."

- How have you dealt with a difficult boss or colleague, one who doesn't listen to you, or has a temper or bad attitude?

This is a bit of a trap. Avoid talking about how you tangle with a boss, especially if you don't know the interviewer and aren't certain exactly what they're trying to glean from your answer. Regardless, they're trying to get some sense of how you relate to authority. It's dangerous because you don't know if they'll be happy to hear how you challenge authority, speaking truth to power, or would prefer to hear you talk about your diplomatic skills. Play the odds and go for how you dealt with a difficult colleague or peer. In both cases, though, it's vital that you paint yourself as the adult who eventually resolved the problem by being reasonable, rational and thoughtful. Split the difference, showing how you used both direct communication and diplomacy to resolve the problem. Nearly all of us has had to deal with a pain in the ass colleague. If you ever had open conflict, mention it, but downplay it – especially your own reaction to it. If you didn't ever have such a situation, say that. Don't ever lie. Instead, talk about how you think you would resolve a conflict like that, if it happened.

- How have you handled a challenging or difficult situation, where the odds were against your achieving the results you were asked to achieve? Or give an example of how you deal with adversity at work.

Steer the interviewer back to your CV. If you've followed my method, you'll have multiple anecdotes to share from your job-experience bullets. Use one that you haven't previously used at this interview.

- Do you work better on your own, or do you prefer collaboration?

Some companies will ask candidates to take a Briggs-Myers personality test. It's fairly exhaustive and tells you and the would-be employer what sort of personality you have – introverted, extroverted, team player, lone wolf, etc, etc. What you're being asked is an armchair version of that test. Are you an introverted loner, or an extroverted team player. Unless you are very clearly one or the other, I'd counsel again splitting the difference, especially if you're going for a managerial or other senior leadership role.

If you like to work on your own, say that and explain why – it's more efficient, faster sometimes to get things done – but qualify it by saying it's situational. And when you find that collaboration is the best way to get a task or project done, that's what you do, and you're comfortable doing it. You are pragmatic, good with people and are always looking for the strongest way to achieve a result.

And then, if you're in a managerial role, or seeking one, explain how you take it upon yourself to focus on team-building and trust, which come with collaboration. You're saying your approach to handling projects is on a case-by-case basis and your mind is flexible, not locked into one approach or another.

- This job isn't a natural fit for your skill set. What makes you think you'll be capable of doing it?

Unless you're applying to something completely out of your area, I'd treat this question as a bit inflammatory and push back gently to ask the interviewer to clarify what, specifically, about your skill set doesn't fit the job. You may find that you didn't read the job ad's fine print, or the interviewer's understanding of your background and skills is flawed. If it's the former, good to hear what you didn't factor in and formulate a plausible answer about how you have the core set of skills, but will focus on developing the one thing you have somewhat less experience at, and that it shouldn't hinder you, because you learn fast, etc, etc. If it's the latter, use it as an opportunity to be corrective and answer by plugging your own skills, leaving no doubt with the interviewer that you do, indeed, possess what's needed to do the job.

- Where do you see yourself in five years?

I've yet to find a single person who's doing exactly what they said they wanted to be doing five years later, so this one is fairly open-ended and pie in the sky. I don't recommend going too crazy with it: Don't say you expect to be CEO in five years, but if you envision a robust career rise, starting with the job you're applying for, it's fair for you to say you would like to be running the team you'll be working on or being a young VP managing multiple teams after learning and acquiring great skills from great bosses at this great company.

If your interests are going to take you from the marketing job you want to have now into scriptwriting or being a museum curator, I suggest keeping that to yourself. You want to use the opportunity to show you are ambitious, have high expectations that come from working hard and achieving strong results and want to climb within the system. Otherwise, if you plan to bank your pay and move off into something else in a couple years, you raise questions about why you're there or why they should hire you.

- If we picked someone else for this job, would you consider another role at our company?

Also tricky, because it makes you wonder whether you're actually still in the running, so I'd start by smiling, nodding and asking, "are you saying you've already picked someone else for the job or have a more-suitable candidate for the role?" Rock the interviewer back on their heels for a bit. Let them assure you that they haven't or explain to you where they are in the process. It's too good an opportunity for you to pass up seeking clarification.

And then, I would say to them, "I'd consider it, depending on its level of seniority, responsibilities and compensation," because you do not want them to bait-and-switch you with a lower-ranking, lower-paying job. And if they do say you might be more suitable as a senior manager than the assistant director role for which you're applying, for example, I'd ask them what skills they think you're lacking that would qualify you for the higher-ranking role.

Again, a good chance to get some feedback about yourself. Be prepared for hemming and hawing, as a good interviewer won't want to risk giving too much away and face possible litigation if you feel you've been discriminated against in seeking the role. But definitely ask what that other role would be and why they think you might be better-suited for it.

- If you got this job, what would your plan be to set yourself, and the company, up for success in the first several months?

This is the "what-is-your-90-day-plan" question. Answer it wisely, but not with a ton of specifics. At this stage in the process, you don't really know enough about what issues the company or team face in your area and how much power, authority and responsibility you'd have to make things better or take them in a different direction – and if so, in which direction.

I would answer by saying your general standard operating procedure is to come in, take a couple weeks to assess the situation, talk to all key internal stakeholders, understand their priorities and pain points, then craft a plan to address the pain points and improve things, based on those priorities.

Say that by 90 days, you'd expect for at least the two or three top-line issues to be resolved by then, with the others to follow shortly thereafter, along with other problems you might have uncovered. And that you would look to put in place a plan for the next six to 12 months after that. Emphasize that you will be learning on the fly and moving at great speed, being focused, but also being flexible enough to adapt the focus to new issues that arise or changing priorities, based on internal or market circumstances. Keep it fairly high level, but make sure they know you know how to do short- and medium-term planning.

- Can you share a situation where you were wrong, or made a mistake, that hurt your team or your project? How did you deal with that tough situation?

Nobody's perfect, and here, you're being asked to show that you aren't. But you never want to pick a situation where you really mucked something up or did something that really hurt the team, project or company.

Find a small-ish error you made, one where you discovered your own error (always better than the tale where the boss stumbled upon your multimillion-dollar mistake), studied it quickly, figured out what you did wrong, sought help, corrected the mistake and really learned something that you'll never do wrong again.

In short, you want to acknowledge professional imperfection, but note that yours are generally fixable by self-healing measures, self-awareness, collaboration, teamwork, initiative and smarts on your part. And that you never make the same mistake twice.

- You seem to have a knack for overachieving on your KPI and P&L. How can we be sure that will be the case here? Do you offer any guarantees? And what should we do with you if you don't overachieve here, as you have elsewhere?

I've used the line that in Major League Baseball, when a batter hits successfully from a safe hit three times out of ten, he's considered all-star caliber. That means he fails 70% of the time. And that I can guarantee I'll surely do better than an MLB all-star for the company in achieving my KPI and helping achieve its P&L targets.

It's kind of jokey, but also making the serious point that you can only do the best you can with your KPI, with experience, contacts, internal situation, politics and other unknowns potentially holding you back at first. Make the point that the longer you're there, the longer you see the problems and issues, the faster, more-efficiently and better you can resolve them. I would also note that the longer you work on, or head up, a team, the better you'll get – and draw on previous work experience and achievements to back that up.

Don't get pulled into a game of trash-talking or posturing before you really know what you're getting into, i.e. don't risk promising overperformance, especially before you even have the job.

How to Prepare for Your Remote Interview

Now that you've prepped your questions, read up on the interviewer and the company, you're ready and raring to go for your remote or in-person interview.

In terms of a remote interviews, this may sound fairly obvious, but wear pants or a skirt/dress. Do not ever sit for a remote job interview in your underwear. A fire drill at home, a surprise visitor or something else that makes you stand up abruptly, and you become an internet meme and a cautionary tale by that company's HR department about why you should never do a Zoom interview in your underwear.

With that out of the way, next up is location. Pick a good, quiet spot to do your interview, one where you won't be constantly disturbed by people or noise. That's also distracting to the interviewer. Sit on a comfortable chair, one where you won't fidget a lot, which sends bad signals to those watching you. Sit up straight, but remember to breathe. You need to look upright, not slumping or leaning forward on the edge of your chair or with your elbows on a desk or tabletop. Turn on your camera without being connected to Zoom, or do a test Zoom of your own and take some screenshots to see how you look when you're sitting upright, comfortably on your chair.

I want to discourage you from using fake backgrounds, no matter how clever or innovative you think you're being. Interviewing with NASA for a job with a background that puts you on the Moon or floating between Jupiter and Saturn sounds cool, but those backgrounds still generally suck, cutting off your hands or other body parts as you move them or lean forward and back. Use the actual background of the room you're in, clearing away clutter and anything inappropriate or unsafe for work. But, by all means, in 100% of the interviews you do, use the "blur" function. You want the interviewers to focus on you, not the Lucky Cat's waving arm just over your shoulder, or the Mickey Mouse clock on your wall.

To continue with the theme of all things technical, neither you nor the interviewer are likely to be IT people (unless you are applying for an IT job and are an IT specialist, yourself). But, anyway, think about your audio-visual situation with your computer well before your interview and test things out, even if you need to practice with friends and family who are somewhere else. You don't want any nasty surprises that harm, limit or delay your interview or leave the interviewers with a bad impression of you and your resourcefulness and ability to use technology.

Test your camera, test your speakers if you're not using any headphones or earphones. And let me share my "wired" rule with you: If you have wired stuff, use it, not wireless or Bluetooth stuff. Wifi bandwidth can fluctuate widely, cutting off or slowing down a video feed, causing it to be laggy or buggy. Bluetooth headphones and earbuds can experience interference that means you lose part of what's being said, and Bluetooth microphones may cut out or reduce the quality of sound when you're talking.

If you have a Wifi router, buy an ethernet cable and an adapter for your computer, if it doesn't have an ethernet port built-in, and get the full bandwidth of your internet connection. You'll get smoother, faster video and audio. Same thing, a pair of bulky headphones or the original wired earphones that came with your smartphone might not be as sexy-looking as Airpods, but those wired options don't need to be charged and deliver full-fidelity sound.

And your microphone is best when it's plugged directly into the computer. Many of you will end up using your Mac or PC's built-in microphone. Test it first and play it back to yourself to hear how you will sound to someone listening to you remotely. You may look very low-tech, but the point of the interview is to answer questions in a way that impresses the interviewer. Chances are you're already nervous about the interview. The last thing you need is a technical problem that gets in the way of being impressive or throwing you off your messages.

You should be sitting in your comfortable spot, ready to go at least five minutes ahead of your interview time. Already try to log on a minute or two before the scheduled time, even if you have to wait for the host to let you in. Don't show up on the dot without having tested your setup previously. If you haven't tested your tech well before the interview, you risk being late and leaving a bad impression with the interviewer, even if you explain you were having tech problems and apologize. A resourceful, thoughtful, mature job-seeker would have thought of all of the potential problems ahead of time and overcome them, but you didn't. Don't be that person.

Live Interviews & Interview Etiquette

If you're going to a live interview, there are a few key rules and bits of etiquette you should follow. First, being on time means you're late. Know where you're supposed to be going well ahead of actually going there by looking at a Google or Apple map and plan your route. Show up 10-15 minutes ahead of your interview in the clothes and shoes you're going to interview in. I'll offer some clothing tips below, but not too many, because they're both a personal choice and out of my sweet spot.

You'll either be asked to sit in a waiting area or be taken into your interview room first. Be polite to the person who welcomes you or directs you to the waiting area. Before the interview starts, clear your mind, work on breathing deeply to relax. The interview process can be tense and make you nervous, tightening your vocal cords and making you talk a half-pitch higher than you normally would.

When your interviewers appear on camera, smile and greet them. If you're doing an in-person interview and sitting in a waiting room and they come to get you, stand up, smile, make eye contact and introduce yourself. Shake hands firmly, but not with a death grip. If you're already in the interview room, stand up, smile and walk around the table to shake hands firmly with the interviewer or interviewers. Handshakes can make an impression, good or bad, an easy smile makes the interviewer feel you are confident, and the eye contact is good to begin building rapport with the interviewer.

What to Wear at Your Remote and Live Interviews

Apart from my initial pants recommendation, I'm going to tread lightly here, because I'm neither a tailor nor a style diva. But here are some basic guidelines. Dress conservatively in most cases. If you're doing a remote, don't wear stripes or anything that might strobe or look weird in different lighting. Solid, pastel colors or white for your shirt. If you're going for a bank or insurance company interview, wear a dark blue or black suit with matching jacket and pants, maybe a conservative tie, not too crazy a pattern, in a shade of medium-to-dark blue. Red is a power color. Avoid it in a tie. Wear a suit jacket over khaki pants, or if it's a startup or Gen-Z-ish company, clean blue jeans without any rips or stains might be OK. Wear brown or black leather shoes, not sneakers. Wear socks.

For women, same approach. Dress in darker colors, a skirt that covers your knees, dress, shirt or blouse that covers your belly button. Maybe a blazer over your shirt. Wear socks or stockings. Overall, if in doubt, think, "office clothes," skewing slightly toward the more-formal for the interview. You can always dress down after you get the job. It's much harder to have to change opinions because you wore your sweet, green Chuck Taylor sneakers with your black suit for the interview. The interviewer will generally accept someone who is a bit overdressed as a sign you're showing respect toward them and the process, that you take them seriously. When you're dressing for a live interview, make sure you aren't sitting on the back of your blazer or suit coat when you sit down, because it's quite tight and uncomfortable.

Get Ready for the Live or Remote Meet & Greet

If you're live, sit down on the chair and get comfortable and settle yourself before you signal you're ready. If you don't have water in front of you, get some if you're doing a Zoom, or ask for some, if you're interviewing in person. You're going to be talking a lot if the interviewer is good, so you'll need some lubrication for your vocal cords.

Be ready to introduce yourself. This is what you've been waiting for – a chance to hit it out of the park talking about your favorite subject: YOU! This is where you roll out the even-longer version of your LinkedIn "About" profile, using about 60 seconds to introduce yourself. Tell the interviewer who you are, where you're from, what you do, what you've achieved and what you want to achieve for their company in the role you're interviewing for. Roll out your adjectives, skills and accomplishments. Let the interviewer know what makes you great and unique, all in a lively tone, without sounding like you're arrogant or bragging.

Check Your Energy Levels

This is one of the most-important things you can do at an interview, whether in-person or remote. Why does your energy level matter? Because, up to now, everything the interviewer knows about you is on a piece of paper. Great writers can be listless interviewers, turning the company's initially positive view about you and your skills and attitude into disappointment and failure to pass through to the next round because you couldn't project the passion and enthusiasm you had on your résumé. You could also be too hyped-up, sending out fidgety, impatient or other negative-energy signals that put the interviewer off.

You need to go into the interview or interview room confident and full of positive energy. You need to project that energy in a way that's felt, believed and appreciated by your interviewer. That means you need to have already thoroughly prepared, researched the company, thought about the questions you'll be asked, how you'll answer and what messages and anecdotes you want to deliver about yourself as you present your professional narrative.

If you don't have all of that squared away, you're going to eat up your own energy and come across as sluggish or downbeat. If you try to push the levels higher because you know you're projecting low, you increase the chances you'll sound frantic or stressed, which won't play well with the interviewer. Bottom line is if you know everything you want to say about yourself, you can spend the interview time trying to be and sit comfortably, get a good read on the interviewer and answer the questions you're asked with the appropriate energy level to impress and get waved into the next round.

In fact, it's often harder to get the energy levels right at remote interviews because you're lacking the actual human contact, making it hard for you to "read the room" or cue off of body language and facial expressions. Humans are social animals, and it's tough to know how to adjust your behavior and energy level when you're lacking actual eye contact. That makes it tougher to connect with the interviewer. And if multiple people are interviewing you, you'd normally shift your gaze and lock eyes with each of the interviewers for a second or two, something you can't do over Zoom.

There's not much you can do about that, except to imagine that you're gazing into the eyes of an interviewer – but only for a second or two, not creepily – as you're phrasing your answers. But you also need to realize that normal people almost always project less energy on camera than they do in person. Ever watch a TV news program and wonder why the anchors sound so "professional?" If you were in the studio during the broadcast, you'd probably say they sounded somewhat cartoonish, "punching" their words too much, being a bit too loud and animated. That's because, while the camera may add 10 pounds, it takes away 20% of your energy, and you will want to replace that to sound energetic while "on air" at your job interview.

Speak a touch louder than you normally do, use your hands, not like karate chops, but to add energy, while answering questions, use facial expressions, smiles, frowns, etc, to punctuate what you're saying and punch key words in your sentences to provide emphasis from a distance to the words and concepts you want the interviewer to know you find important. Be a bit cartoonish. It's unlikely you'll be so cartoonish that you come across like a freak, but do test out your "remote-interview voice" with family and friends before you do it live with a company recruiter. You can always dial things down or up slightly. What you want is for the person you're testing it on to tell you that you sound natural and believable as they listen to you online.

Don't punch things up too much in an in-person interview or you definitely will come across as a freak. But you do want to project energy and emotion during the interview. Nobody feels comfortable interviewing a zombie. If you're sitting in a chair or on a couch, lean forward, but just a bit, use your hands from the wrists, not moving the whole arm or forearm, to gesture and emphasize the words you want to stick in the interviewer's mind. It's OK to lean back in your chair and cross your legs conservatively, nod along with the interviewer's question and be a bit more passive while listening, but you want to raise the energy level when you're answering questions. It's not just leaning forward, gesturing or punching words, though.

You also want to be aware of what type of energy and signals you're sending. For example, if you've practiced your anecdotes enough, you'll have parts of it where you want to smile and get the interviewing smiling about something funny that's about to some. If you're passionate about what you've achieved, make the interviewer feel that. You can sometimes see from facial expressions and body languages if the interviewer has cued off of your humor, passion or other emotions you're trying to project from your anecdotal answer to their question. Remember, you've probably answer this question many more times than they've asked it, and it's in your own words, it's your own story. So, you should OWN the anecdote and the emotions and energy with which you deliver it.

Wrapping Your Interview with the Q&A

Once you've been grilled by the interviewer, it's your turn to grill them. Expect a five-to-10-minute Q&A session, where the interviewer turns to you and says, "feel free to ask me any questions!"

At the same time you prepared for the questions you expected to be asked by your interviewer, you should be drawing up three good questions for your interviewer about the job or the company. Don't ask things you can find via Google. Do leave your questions open-ended, make the focus "softer," or ask about things like company culture so you give yourself a breather and the interviewer a chance to explain the job and company to you in more detail from an insider's view.

Don't ask about pay or other compensation at a job interview. That can wait until a formal offer comes in. In the same vein, many companies will ask you, on your job applications, to tell them your salary expectations, or they provide a figure to you or ask what you're making now. Just don't go there. Deflect by saying you're sure you and the company will reach a suitable agreement once they are sure they want you.

Lastly, ask the interviewer to talk about themself. Most people love to talk about themselves. Ask them about their career journey, and if it's normal, and if you can expect to have a similar upward trajectory should you stay there for a number of years. Apart from learning things and gaining insight into a career at the company, you also bring yourself closer to the interviewer, who will think you're quite thoughtful for asking them about their own career.

What's Next?

Let's say you've really crushed your first interview. What happens next? Typically, you won't hear from your interviewer that day whether or not you've made it to a next round. But it's fair for you to ask in the Q&A session when – and how – you can expect to hear whether you've made it, or what the next steps are.

Companies that took the time to invite you in for an interview will usually inform you about whether you made it to the next round, or issue you a polite, formal, written rejection note, often with some encouragement. If you don't get an answer at the interview and don't hear from the interviewer or company within a few days, you should ping the interviewer with an email, again asking when they expect to get back to you.

If you do hear from the company that you're through to the next round, don't let grass grow under your feet. There are two types of interviewees. The ones who come in with some decent research and knowledge, a good manner and approach, and do fantastic in their first interview, but then plateau, don't put in any more work or research. They start to look flat in the second round, and even if they make it to a third or final round, they fall short because they have done nothing to get better, get deeper or show more interest in the job and company. It's such a shame to have gotten your CV and first interview right, but then fade because of laziness or lack of care in prepping for future rounds.

And then, there are the superstars, who make it through to the second round and put in hours more of Google research, who contact peers at the company to talk about their own experiences (and share them with the interviewers to show you put in the effort) and who get smarter and more-focused each time they sit down with a new interviewer. These are the ones who impress and achieve a consensus "this is the one" status from all the interviewers as they're polled by HR about who gets the eventual job offer. You want to be that person. Keep making yourself smarter about the job and company, keep asking better, sharper questions, keep nailing and honing the telling of your professional narrative.

Last thing I want to tell you is to never get down or discouraged in the long, often fruitless, job search process. After reading this ebook, you understand there's a whole process involved, that you are always a work in progress, that you and your narrative fit into a broader ecosystem. You may be the white whale who submits a single, cold application and gets the job, or you may have to apply to 100 jobs before you get an offer. Use each application as a chance to better and sharpen your presentation and understanding of the career ecosystem, remember rejection is seldom personal and that you only need to come out of the process with one job.

I'm not trying to upsell, but if you feel you want or need deeper or more-personalized help and coaching in any of the steps you take to get a job, I'm here to provide paid consultation at a reasonable rate. I'll make time for you and tailor suggestions and proposed solutions for you. I can take you through mock interviews, simulate the pressure, help you feel more-comfortable in dealing with tough questions.

I can never guarantee you success, but I hope what you just read will resonate with you and help you gather your thoughts, prepare and act more knowledgeably and confidently. And if we go further, and I hear from you about coaching sessions online, I can promise you I'll always do my best to make you and your narrative and job search better.

Adam S. Najberg

About the Author

Adam Najberg is a communications and content professional who has lived and worked all over the world. He spent the first 25 years of his career as a reporter and editor, mostly at The Wall Street Journal and Dow Jones Newswires. He began his career with The Associated Press in San Francisco and wrote for nearly a dozen publications as a freelance contributor. He has been a recruiter and hiring manager since 1997. He has mentored or advised nearly 150 people, from entry level to the executive suite, on their career options and direction. That has helped them gain a broader perspective on the job-search process and the path they choose to take. His holistic approach involves helping job-seekers to craft a unique, personalized narrative, assess and classify their top attributes and skills to stand out in the recruitment and interview process.

www.ingramcontent.com/pod-product-compliance
Lightning Source LLC
Chambersburg PA
CBHW051343150726
48000CB00003B/1020